American Muscle Cars
1960-1975

Bruce LaFontaine

DOVER PUBLICATIONS, INC.
Garden City, New York

About the Author

Bruce LaFontaine is the writer and illustrator of 35 nonfiction books created for the children's middle-reader (ages 8–12) and adult markets. He specializes in the subject areas of history, science, transportation, and architecture. His published works include *Modern Experimental Aircraft, Famous Buildings of Frank Lloyd Wright, Great Inventors and Inventions*, and many others. His 1999 book, *Exploring the Solar System*, was selected by Astronomy magazine as one of the 21 best astronomy books for children. He is included in *Something About the Author*, and the *International Biographical Centre Who's Who of Authors*, publications profiling prominent authors and illustrators. Mr. LaFontaine has worked in the Rochester, New York, area as a writer, illustrator, and art director for 25 years.

Bibliographical Note

American Muscle Cars, 1960–1975, is a new work, first published by
Dover Publications, Inc., in 2001.

International Standard Book Number

ISBN-13: 978-0-486-41863-6
ISBN-10: 0-486-41863-4

Manufactured in the United States by LSC Communications
41863421   2020
www.doverpublications.com

Introduction

During the 1960s and early '70s, a unique class of American automobile was introduced, became wildly popular, and then faded from the scene. These vehicles were given the nickname "muscle cars" in deference to their powerful engines and blazingly fast acceleration. *American Muscle Cars, 1960–1975* depicts this exciting era in automotive history.

Most of the muscle cars in this book had large V-8 engines generating over 300 horsepower; a few exceeded 400 horsepower. The size and power of muscle car engines are measured in "cubic-inch displacement" (cid) and "horsepower" (hp). Generally speaking, the greater the cubic-inch displacement, the higher the horsepower rating. Cubic-inch displacement is a measure of how much empty air volume is created by the engine cylinder bores—the holes in which the pistons slide up and down during combustion. The length of travel of the piston in the cylinder also affects cubic-inch size. One of the most popular V-8 engines used in many muscle machines displaced 350 cubic-inches. Other elements that can increase horsepower are the number and size of the carburetors—the carburetor being the device that fuels the engine—and the relative efficiency of direct fuel-injection systems. Other factors, such as compression ratios of the combustion cycle; high-performance engine parts such as valves, camshafts, exhaust/intake manifolds; and free-flow exhaust systems also helped generate higher horsepower ratings.

Muscle cars were available in many types and sizes. In their early years, most of these dynamic machines were the largest full-size vehicles offered by a car manufacturer and were equipped with the most powerful engines available. The exception is the Corvette, a small two-seat sports car built by Chevrolet beginning in 1953. The Corvette remains one of the last of the breed. As the muscle car era continued, mid-size cars were also built with high-horsepower engines, gradually overtaking the bigger vehicles in popularity. But the bulk of the muscle car years was filled by the "pony" cars, which played off the overwhelming success of the Ford Mustang, introduced in 1964. Within a few years, every major auto builder was offering these relatively small, lightweight vehicles equipped with big V-8 engines.

In the 100-year history of the automobile, certain types of very popular vehicles have been strongly identified with specific countries or regions. Europe led the way in sports car design and manufacture. Japan would eventually take first place in the production of fuel-efficient compact cars. But muscle cars were the exclusive province of the United States, where technology has always been highly esteemed, and where the automobile—one of technology's supreme off-shoots—has always been a special object of fascination. As a result of the remarkably dynamic, creative American economy and culture, this classic series of automobiles was produced for the relatively short span of fifteen years. Although they are no longer built in the hundreds of thousands as they were during their heyday, well-maintained or restored muscle cars have become valuable in today's classic car market. While most of these vehicles originally sold for less than $5,000, some of the most sought-after restored versions now command prices in the $100,000 price range. The muscle car has become a legend in automotive history—a uniquely American contribution to that story.

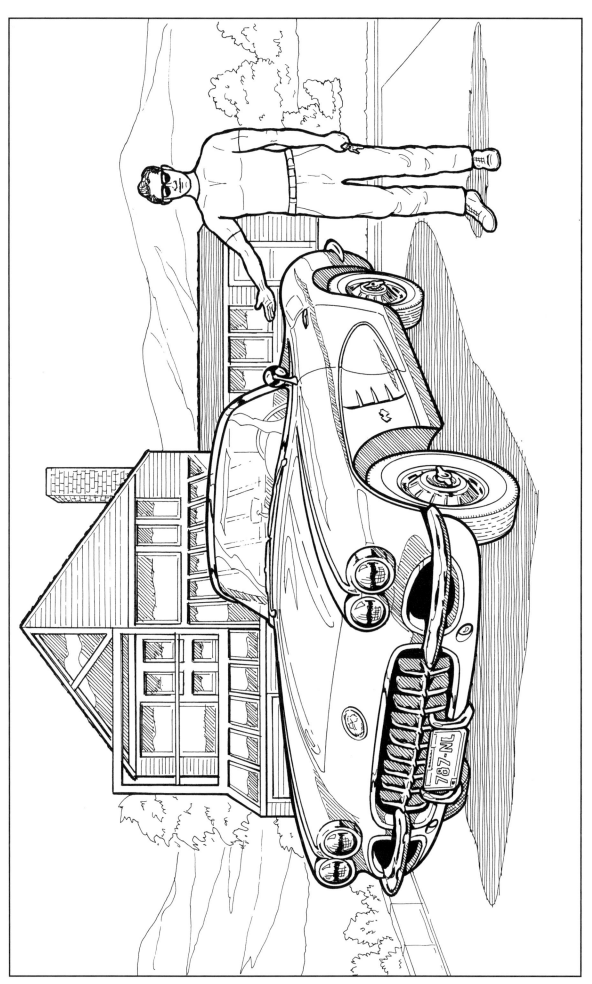

1. 1960 Chevrolet Corvette

Introduced in 1953, the Corvette became America's first sports car. But it was not until the Corvette was equipped with a V-8 engine in 1955 that it could be included in the muscle car family. Initially available with a 265 cubic-inch V-8, it produced a respectable 255 hp. In 1957 the Corvette became one of the fastest production cars on the road with the advent of a new 283 cubic-inch engine and optional fuel injection. With this new combination, the Corvette's power jumped to 283 hp, an amazing rating of one horsepower per cubic-inch. A 1960 model with this powerplant is shown above. By 1962, the Corvette could be equipped with an even bigger 327 cubic-inch engine.

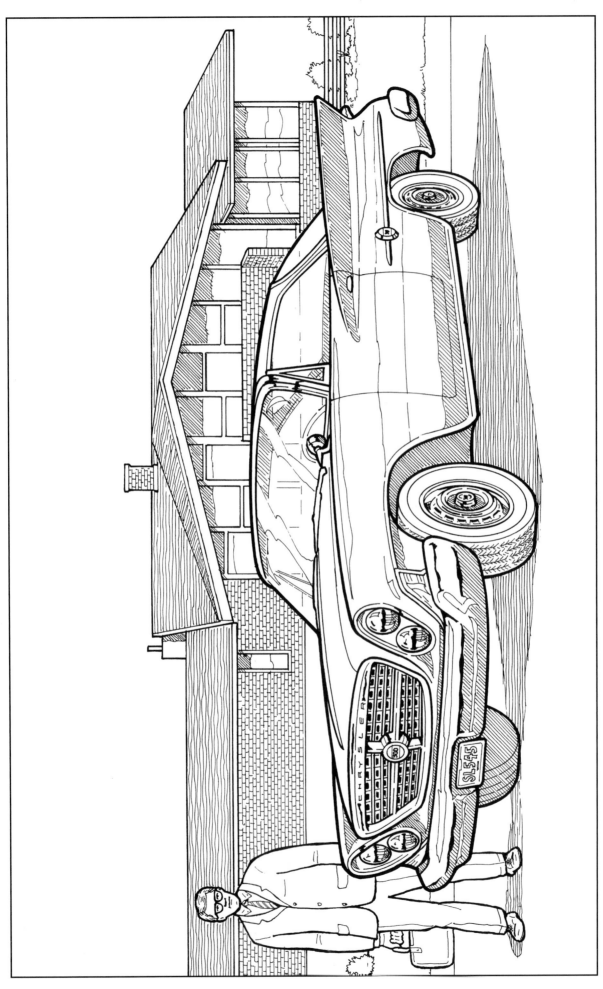

2. 1961 Chrysler 300-G

At the other end of the muscle car size spectrum from the diminutive Corvette was the full-sized Chrysler 300-G 2-door hardtop, pictured above. Almost 19 feet long and weighing 4,500 lbs., this chrome-laden, big-finned beauty nonetheless could move very quickly. It was powered by the potent Chrysler "Max Wedge" 413 cubic-inch engine, developing an impressive 385 hp through dual 4-barrel carburetors. Possessing this massive power cloaked and disguised in the standard Chrysler body, a business executive could assume the role of street racer at any stoplight.

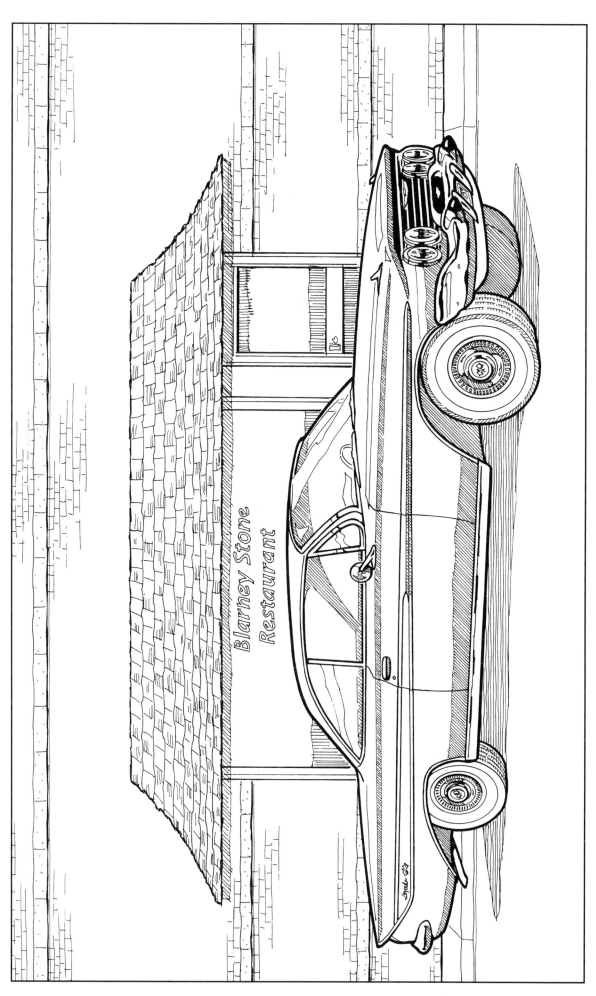

3. 1961 Chevrolet Impala Super Sport (SS)

Chevrolet entered the muscle car arena in a big way with the full-sized Impala Super Sport. This model was equipped with the legendary "409" cubic-inch V-8 made famous by the Beach Boys hit song of that name. The 409 was an enlarged version of Chevy's venerable 348 cubic-inch V-8 of the 1950s. The 1961 Impala Super Sport depicted above was equipped with the 360 hp 409 engine fueled by a single 4-barrel carburetor. A more powerful version of the 409 was offered in 1962, featuring dual 4-barrel carbs. This impressive engine produced 409 hp. By 1963, a monster 425 hp version of the 409 was optional. The 409 was discontinued in 1965, giving way to the equally renowned "427" V-8.

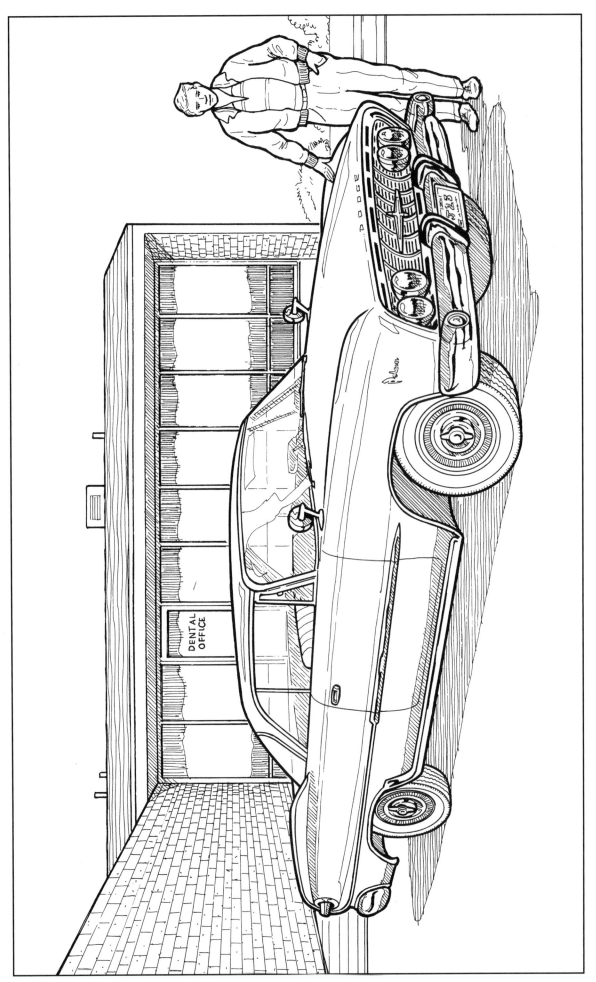

4. 1961 Dodge Polara D-500

The first years of muscle car history were dominated by full-sized, top of the line vehicles from Ford, Chrysler, and General Motors. These cars had a wheelbase of at least 120 inches, measured between 18 and 19 feet in length, and weighed in at around 4,000 lbs. They were powered by the biggest, most powerful V-8 engines available. Depicted here is a Dodge Polara D-500 2-door hardtop. It could be equipped with a 361 cubic-inch V-8 producing 315 hp, or an even more powerful 383 cubic-inch engine pumping out 325 hp. The Dodge/Plymouth "383" engine would go on to become a staple of the Chrysler muscle car lineup of the 1960s and '70s.

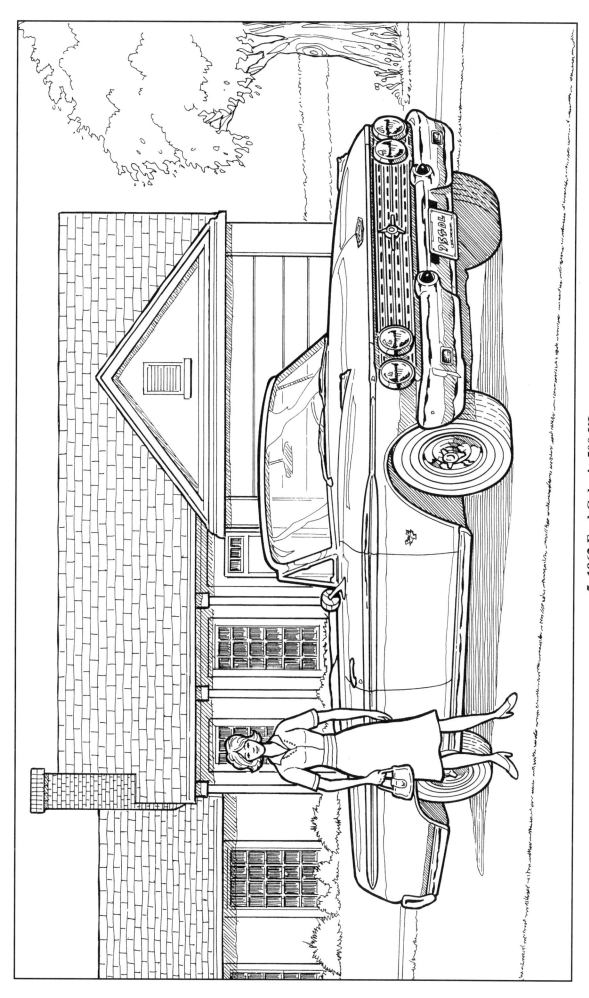

5. 1962 Ford Galaxie 500 XL

Ford Motors' answer to Chevy's popular Impala SS "409" was the Galaxie 500 XL, pictured above in a convertible model. This full-sized muscle car was available in a range of big V-8 engines. Introduced in 1961, the Galaxie 500 was available with a 390 cubic-inch powerplant producing 375 hp and a single 4-barrel carburetor, or with 401 hp using three 2-barrel carbs. In 1962 the Galaxie 500 XL was offered with an engine increased to 406 cubic-inches. Again offered with 2 types of carburetion, the single 4-barrel version kicked out 385 hp, while the triple-carb model produced a mighty 405 hp. Another increase in engine size and power came in 1963 with the introduction of the 427 cubic-inch engine. This powerplant cranked out 410 hp in the three 2-barrel carb version, and 425 hp with twin 4-barrels.

6. 1962 Ford Thunderbird

Ford also answered Chevy's sports car, the Corvette, with their Thunderbird model. The T-Bird was introduced in 1955 as a two-seat sports car intended to compete directly with the Corvette. It continued in this configuration through the 1957 model year. Due to disappointing sales, Ford redesigned the T-Bird in 1958 as a four-seat "personal luxury" vehicle. The 1962 convertible shown above came equipped with a 390 cubic-inch V-8 available with a single 4-barrel carburetor producing 375 hp, or with triple 2-barrel carbs putting out 401 hp. The T-Bird convertible was also offered with a unique molded fiberglass panel called a "tonneau cover." This device formed a smooth, aerodynamic cover extending from the back of the front seats, over the rear seats, and to the edge of the passenger compartment. It gave the effect of possessing a two-seat open sports car.

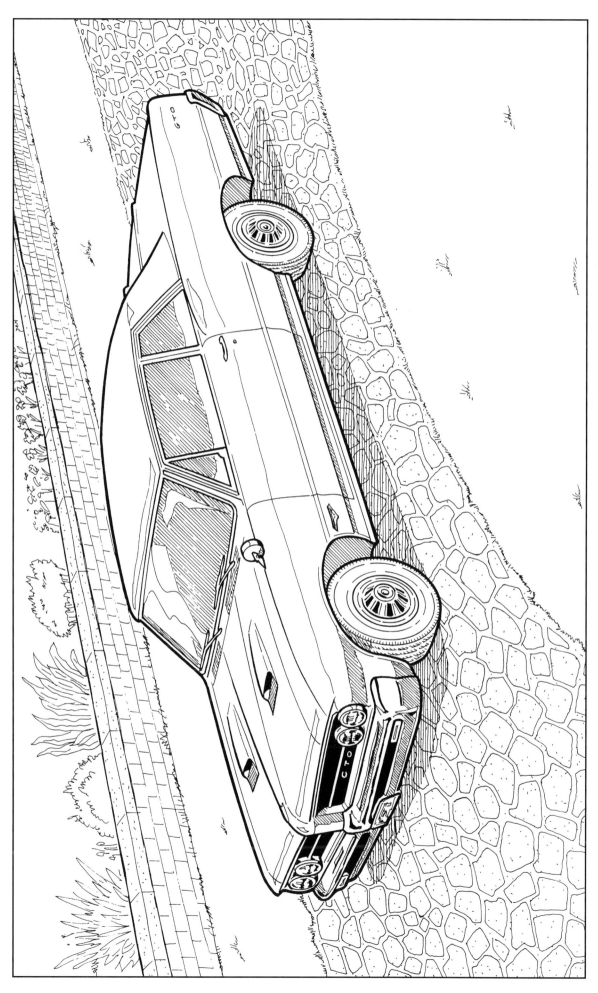

7. 1964 Pontiac Tempest GTO

If any single vehicle could be held responsible for the popularity and success of the muscle car era, it would be the Pontiac GTO. Introduced in 1964, it was built on Pontiac's mid-size body and chassis (frame), the Tempest LeMans. The GTO was the first vehicle to employ less weight, fewer luxury features, and more horsepower as its guiding principles. It came equipped with a 389 cubic-inch engine fed by triple 2-barrel carburetors, producing 348 hp. A four-speed floor shift was standard equipment. With a price well within the reach of the younger generation, the GTO became the car of choice for thousands of speed-loving auto enthusiasts. Its success forced other car manufacturers to come up with their own high-horsepower vehicles, essentially creating the muscle car boom.

8. 1964 Corvette Sting Ray

Chevrolet launched a newly designed version of the Corvette in 1963, the sleek Sting Ray. With its pointed aerodynamic nose and hidden headlights, the Sting Ray was an immediate best-seller. Available with a more powerful 327 cubic-inch engine, introduced in 1962, the Sting Ray continued Corvette's domination of the American sports car and muscle car market. The 327-equipped speedster was available with a range of engine horsepower: Engines with a single 4-barrel carburetor produced either 300 hp or 340 hp. The top of the line fuel-injected 327 was also offered with a potent rating of 370 hp. Although the 327 was the most popular engine to power the Corvette, by 1966 more massive engines were optional, including the famed 396 and 427 cubic-inch brutes.

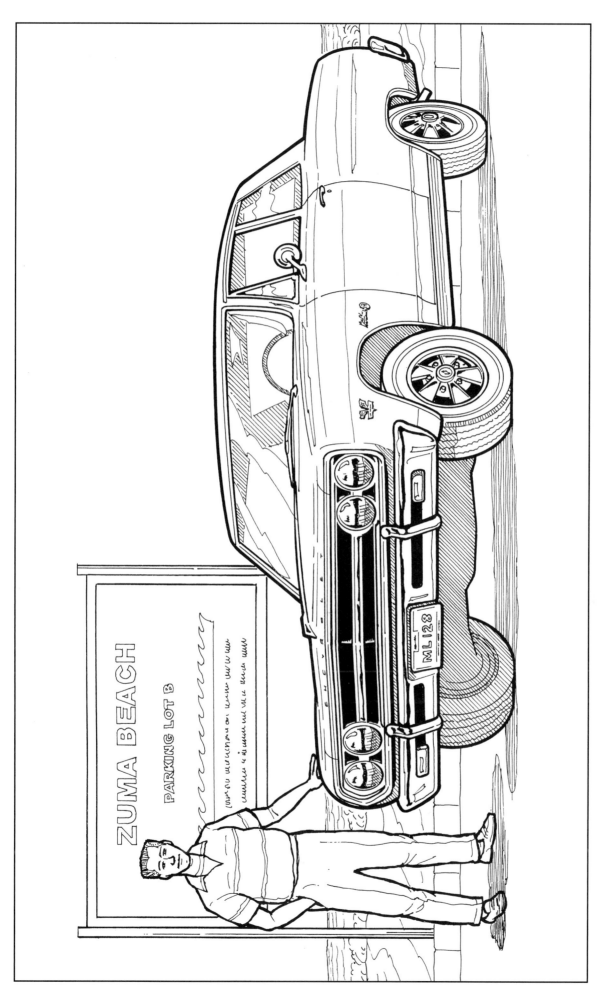

9. 1965 Chevrolet Chevelle Malibu SS 396

Chevy's entry in the mid-size vehicle muscle car field was aimed at luring customers away from the Pontiac GTO. Their 2-door hardtop "Malibu" model of the mid-size Chevelle could be ordered with the "SS" (Super Sport) package and could be equipped with a variety of powerful V-8s. In 1964 the Malibu SS was available with a 327 engine that put out an impressive 300 hp. By 1965 the power of the 327 was upped to 340 hp, and an even larger engine was offered, the muscular 396 cubic-incher. This powerplant gave the machine an enormous 370 hp to propel the relatively lightweight vehicle. The Malibu SS 396 became an instant king of the "stoplight drag race."

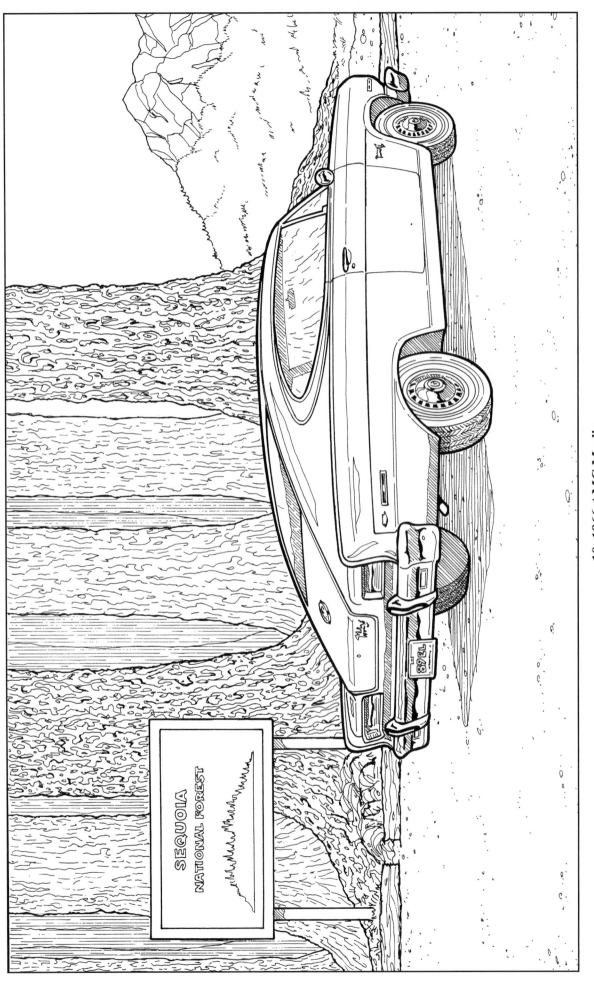

10. 1966 AMC Marlin

The smallest of the American car manufacturers of the muscle car era was American Motors (AMC), makers of the compact Rambler. They made a number of different muscle cars during this period in order to compete with the bigger car companies. In 1966, AMC introduced the Marlin, based on their midsize Rambler Classic body and frame. A sleek fastback roof was grafted on to the 2-door body style, and several V-8 engines were offered. A base engine of 287 cubic-inches and 198 hp was available, but most Marlins came equipped with a more muscular 327 cubic-incher, producing 270 hp. Although the Marlin was not as fast as the other muscle cars and was only built from 1966 to 1968, it remains an interesting effort by the fourth largest automaker.

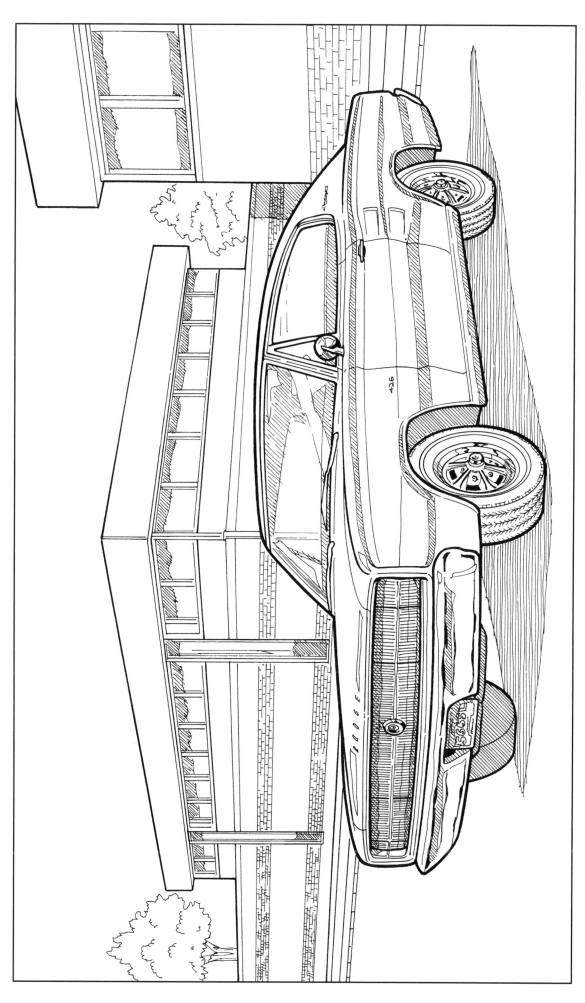

11. 1966 Dodge Charger

Chrysler began their challenge to the GTO with the Dodge Charger, introduced in 1966. Based on the mid-size Dodge Coronet body, the Charger also received a swooping fastback roofline much like the AMC Marlin. However, the Charger could be had with a range of *real* muscle car engines. The 1966 model depicted above could be equipped with a 383 cubic-inch powerplant developing 325 hp, or the legendary 426 "hemi." This massive, powerful 426 cubic-inch engine pumped out *425 hp*, making it one of the most powerful muscle car engines ever produced. The hemi, so called for its hemispherically shaped combustion chambers, proved to be a potent sales and marketing tool for the entire Chrysler muscle car lineup. Along with the 440 cubic-inch engine introduced in 1967, Chrysler offered massive power for the dedicated street racer.

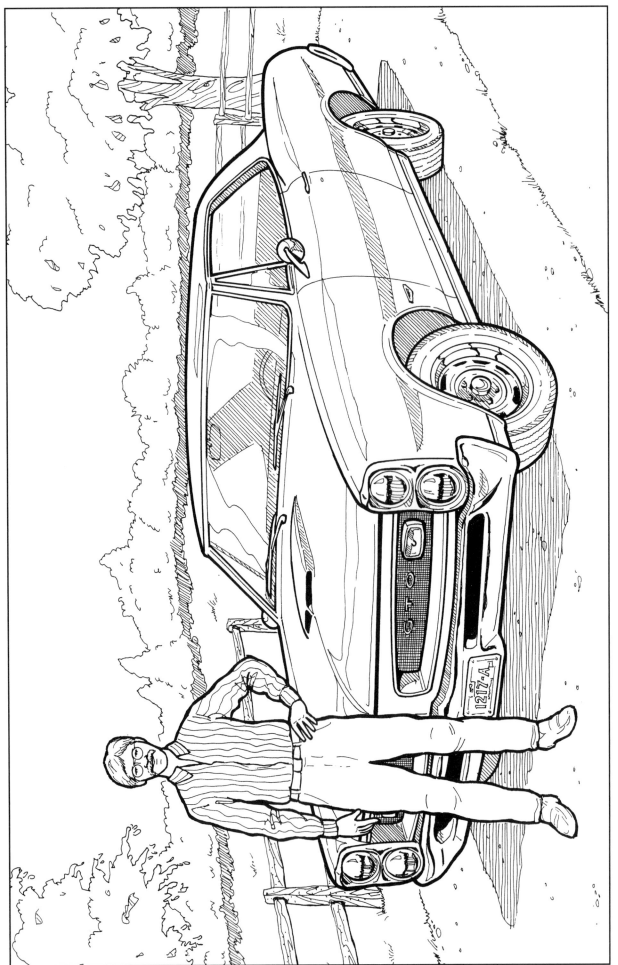

12. 1967 Pontiac Tempest GTO

Pontiac redesigned the popular GTO for 1966/67 to include stylish vertically stacked quad headlights, as shown in the '67 model pictured above. A new 400 cubic-inch engine fueled by a single 4-barrel carburetor, developing 335 hp, was also introduced. Sales for the GTO, nicknamed the "Goat," remained very strong despite competition from the other car manufacturers.

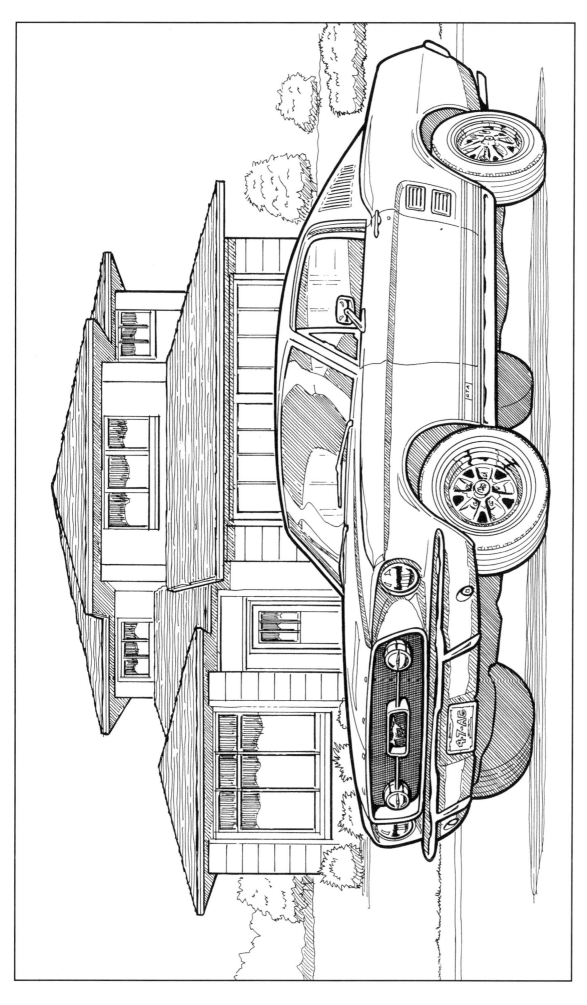

13. 1967 Ford Mustang GT Fastback

The class of muscle cars that followed full-size and mid-size models eventually became the dominant vehicles of the era. These were the "pony" cars, so called for the first of the series, the legendary Ford Mustang. The Mustang was introduced in 1964, available with a 6-cylinder engine or a 289 cubic-inch V-8. As the Mustang's popularity rapidly grew, different versions of the vehicle were offered with a range of engine power. The 1967 Mustang GT shown above could be ordered with a massive 390 cubic-inch V-8 putting out 320 hp. The GT models, equipped with an automatic transmission, were designated GTA's. A limited number of specially modified Mustangs were introduced in 1965—the Shelby Cobra GT series. Built by Texas race car driver and designer Carroll Shelby, the Cobra Mustang GT-350 and GT-500 vehicles became two of the most potent and sought-after muscle cars of the era.

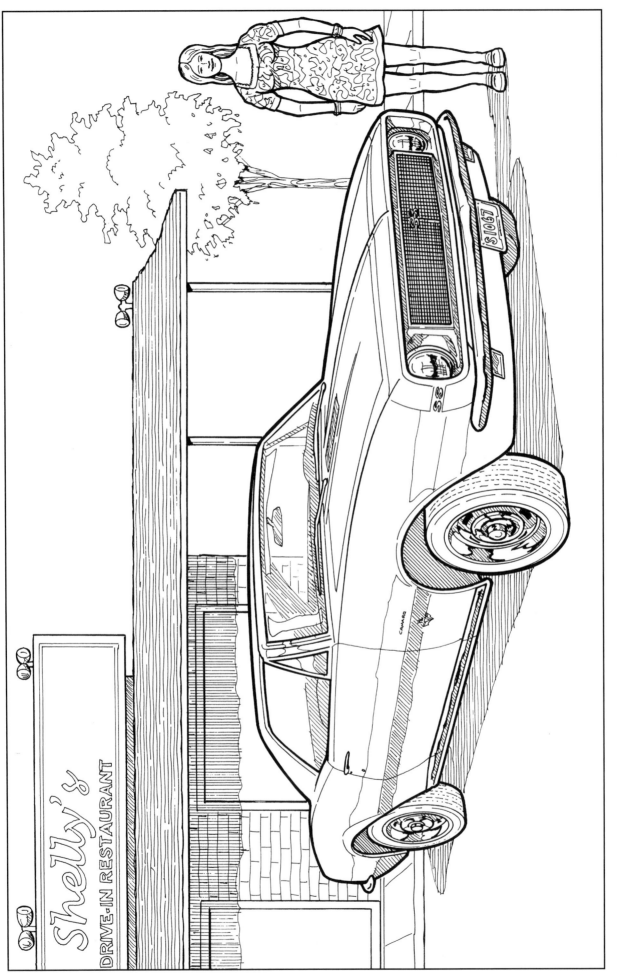

14. 1967 Chevrolet Camaro SS 350/SS 396

Chevrolet reacted to the success of the Mustang with the introduction of the Camaro in 1967. It was available in a number of models, including the RS (Rally Sport) and SS (Super Sport). The RS/SS 350 came equipped with a 350 cubic-inch engine developing 298 hp. The SS 396 was powered by the 396 cubic-incher, pumping out 350 hp. With either engine, the exceedingly fast 3,300 lb. Camaro became a popular, successful competitor to the Mustang and other pony cars of the era.

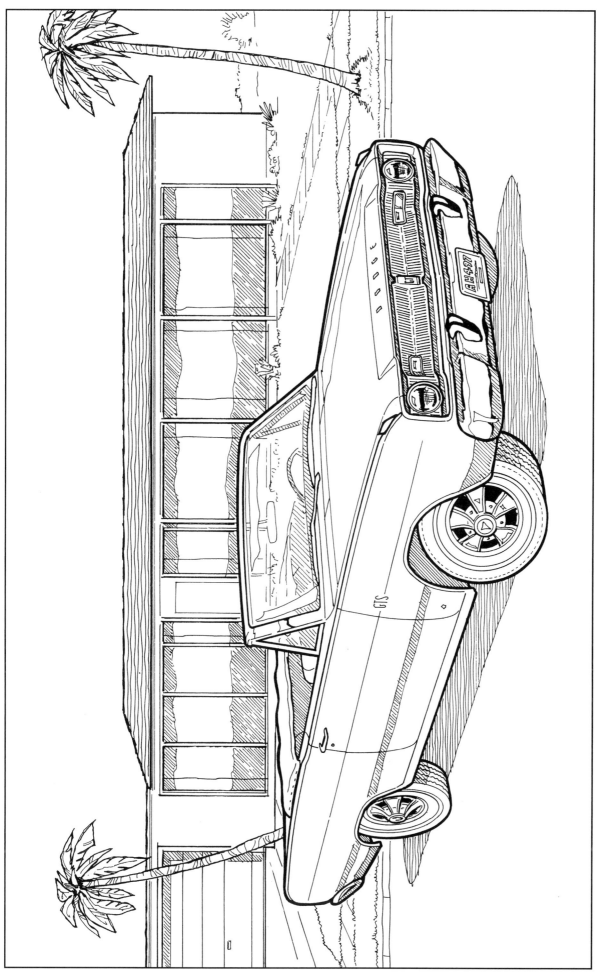

15. 1967 Dodge Dart GTS

Chrysler Motors also entered the muscle car arena in the compact car division. Shown above is a Dodge Dart GTS convertible based on the Dart compact sedan series. The GTS was equipped with a powerful small-block 340 cubic-inch engine putting out a respectable 275 hp. In a vehicle weighing just over 3,000 lbs., this powerplant provided the Dart GTS with very quick acceleration. In 1968, a limited number of GTS models were built with the larger 383 cubic-inch V-8, which developed 330 hp. With that engine the little Dodge Dart became a real muscle car contender.

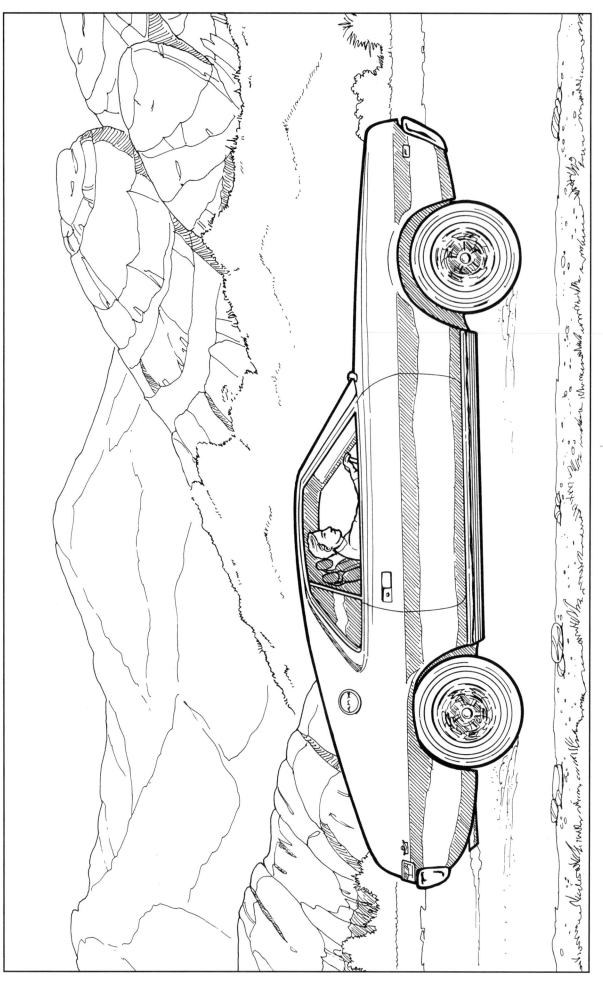

16. 1968 AMC AMX Fastback

The next AMC automobile to compete in the muscle car market was the 2-seat AMX, built from 1968 to 1970. Because of its small size this car was very fast, even when equipped with the base engine, a 290 cubic-inch V-8 putting out 225 hp. When built with the optional larger V-8s, the AMX became a potent boulevard drag racer. It was available with a 343 cubic-inch engine producing 280 hp, or the largest AMC V-8, the 390 cubic-inch powerplant that cranked out 315 hp. Because of their relatively small production numbers, restored AMXs are quite valuable on today's classic car market.

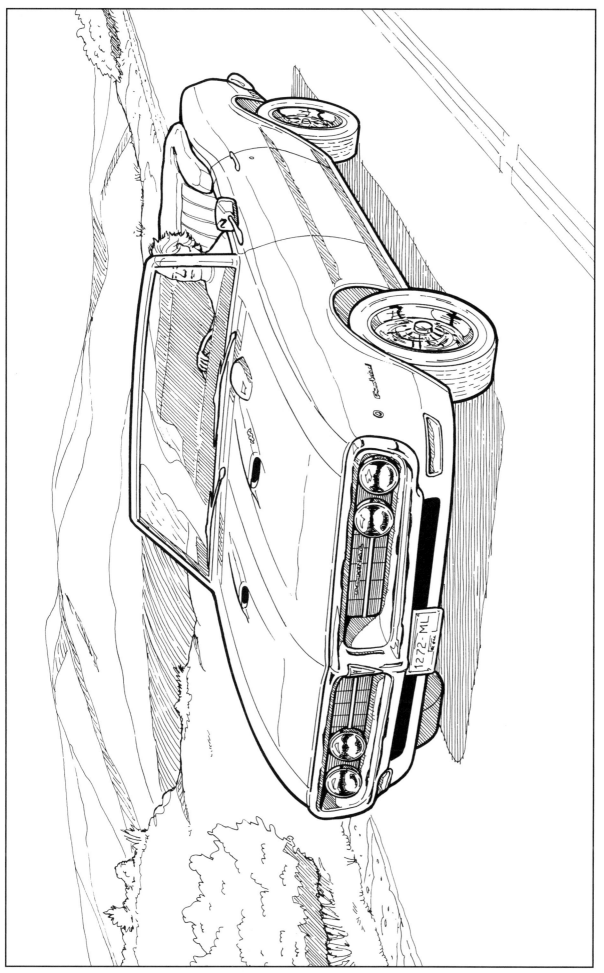

17. 1968 Pontiac Firebird 400

Pontiac joined the pony car league in 1967 with the stylish Firebird, based on the Chevy Camaro chassis/frame. It was initially available with a 326 cubic-inch V-8 producing 285 hp in the optional "HO" (High Output) version. It could also be ordered with a 400 cubic-inch, 325 hp engine. For 1968, the 326 engine was replaced with a 350 cubic-incher producing 320 hp. The '68 Firebird 400 "HO" version depicted above was rated at 335 hp. The successful Firebird became a popular stablemate to the GTO in the muscle car world.

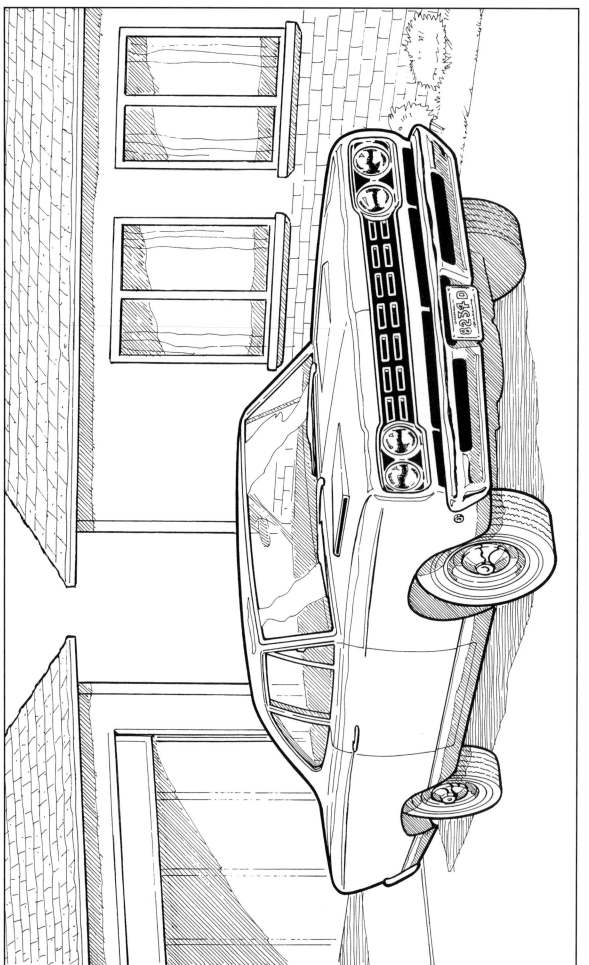

18. 1968 Plymouth Roadrunner

The Plymouth division of Chrysler Motors carved out its own niche in American muscle car lore with its budget-priced rocket, the Roadrunner. With a direct tie-in to Warner Brothers' popular Roadrunner and Coyote cartoon characters, the mid-size muscle machine was powerful, fast, and affordable. Based on the Plymouth Belvedere body and chassis, it offered little in the way of luxury options. The primary selling point was the standard 335 hp, 383 cubic-inch V-8 powerplant. In 1969, the Roadrunner was marketed with the mammoth 440 "six-pack" engine. With its triple 2-barrel carburetors, the 440 pumped out a tremendous 390 hp. Upping the ante again in 1971, the Roadrunner topped out with the optional 426 "hemi" engine, producing an astounding 425 hp.

19. 1968 Mercury Cougar GT-E

Lincoln-Mercury, the high-end luxury car segment of Ford Motors, entered the pony car field in 1967 with the Cougar. It was, essentially, a restyled, upgraded Mustang. The muscle car version was the Cougar GT, initially available with the powerful 390 cubic-inch V-8 producing 320 hp. More power was on tap for 1968, with the limited production "GT-E." This model was equipped with the Ford "427" cubic-inch engine generating 390 hp for the first half of 1968, then with the 335 hp, 428 cubic-inch "Cobra Jet" V-8 in the second half of that year. The Cougar never rang up the sales figures that the Mustang and Camaro/Firebird achieved but was nonetheless a powerful member of the muscle car set.

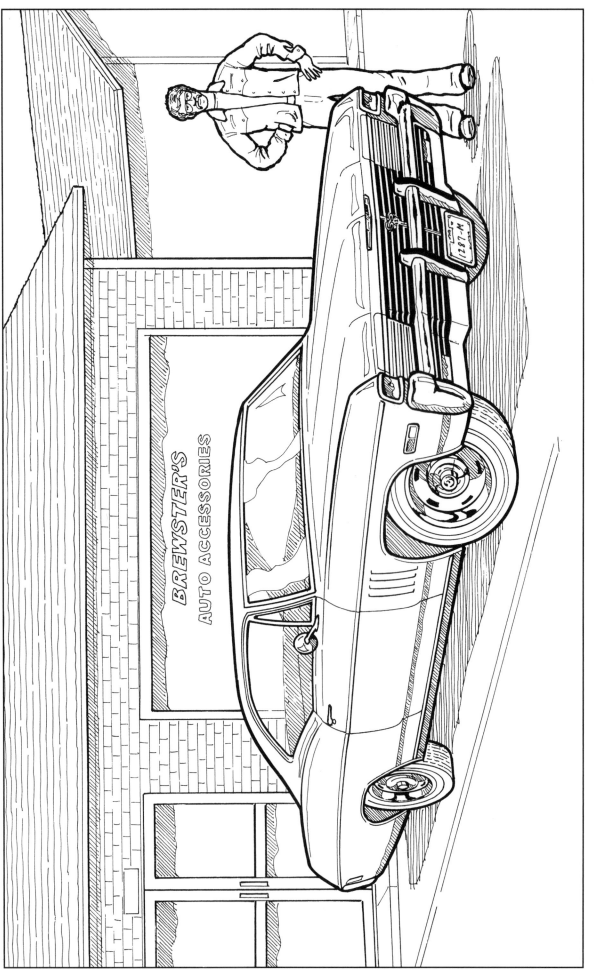

20. 1968 Chevrolet Impala SS 427

The full-size muscle cars manufactured by Chevrolet began with the '61 Impala, equipped with the famous "409" engine; they ended with the 1969 Impala SS powered by the mighty 427 cubic-inch V-8. Shown above in a '68 model, the 427 engine cranked out 385 hp to move the 3,900 lb. Impala SS at a pace much quicker than many smaller, lighter cars. With the end of the big Impala Super Sport models, the muscle car craze became almost exclusively the domain of mid-size vehicles and pony cars.

BREWSTER'S
AUTO ACCESSORIES

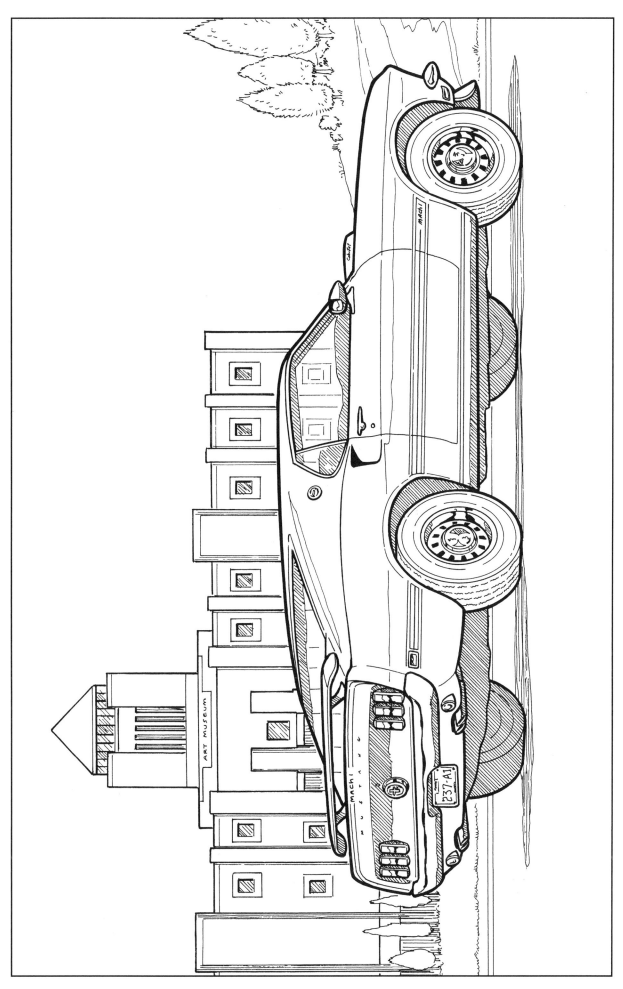

21. 1969 Ford Mustang Mach 1 Cobra Jet

The success of the Mustang generated a variety of muscle car versions of Ford's original pony car. Following the Mustang GT of 1967, the '69 Mach 1 model shown above featured the massive 428 cubic-inch "Cobra Jet" engine rated at 335 hp. This stylish fastback Mustang also came equipped with front air dam and rear deck lid spoiler. In 1970, the Mach 1 was built with the even more powerful 429 cubic-inch Cobra Jet V-8, rated at a potent 370 hp.

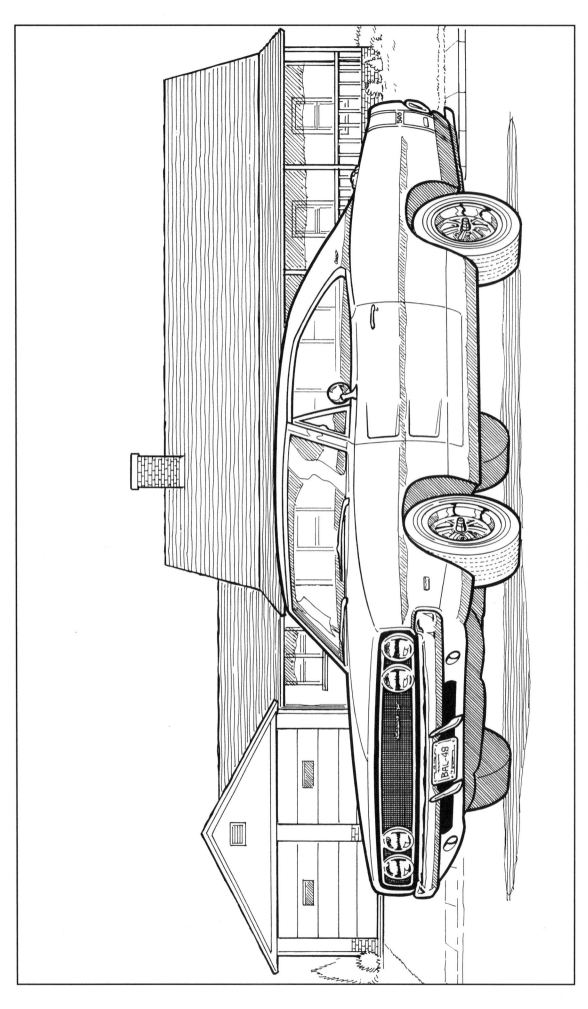

22. 1969 Dodge Charger 500

The Dodge Charger line received a completely restyled body design in 1968—it no longer resembled a thinly disguised Coronet sedan with a fastback top grafted onto it. The smooth and slippery design was an immediate sales success, securing the Charger's position solidly in the mid-size muscle car market. The two top powerplants available were the 440 "six pack" churning out 375 hp, and the 426 "hemi" with its incredible power output of 425 hp. Shown above is the 1969 Charger 500 model, a limited production vehicle designed to allow the Charger to compete more successfully in NASCAR stock car racing. The Charger's normally recessed grille and hidden headlights were replaced by a flush-mounted grille with quad headlamps; the rear tunneled fastback window was also mounted flush to reduce air turbulence at high speed.

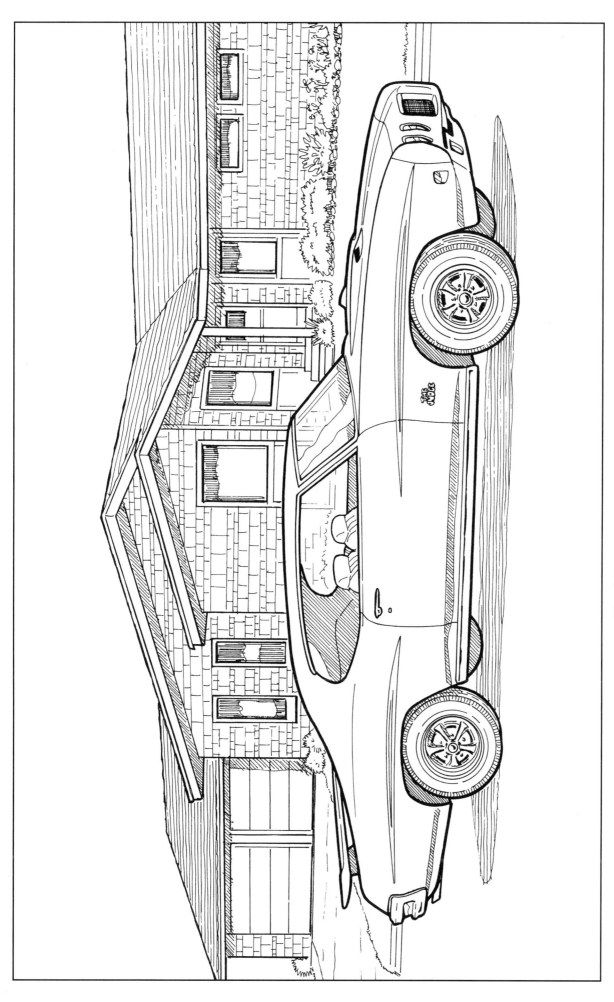

23. 1969 Pontiac Tempest GTO Judge

To spice up the GTO lineup for 1969, Pontiac introduced a limited production version called the Judge. In addition to a colorful bright orange paint job and special striping over the wheel wells, the Judge came equipped with a 400 cubic-inch engine featuring ram air induction for the carburetor. With this setup, the engine churned out a respectable 370 hp. In 1970, the GTO Judge was available with a monstrous 455 cubic V-8 rated at 335 hp. The Judge version of the GTO was discontinued in 1971. Produced in small numbers, this vehicle is a relative rarity in today's classic car market.

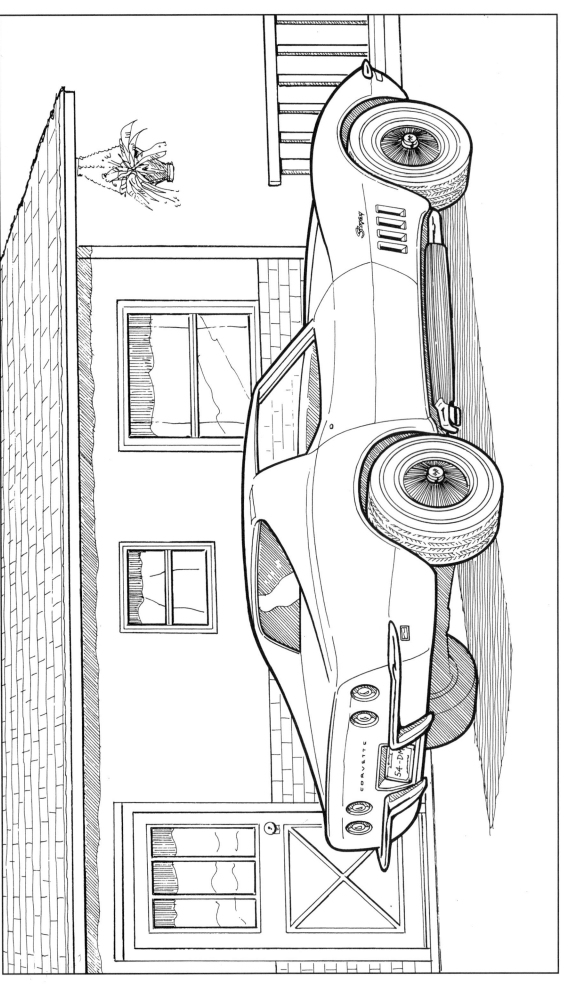

24. 1969 Chevrolet Corvette Stingray

Continuing its success as America's only sports car/muscle car, the Corvette was completely redesigned in 1968. The new vehicle was rechristened the "Stingray," a change from the 1963–67 series of Sting Rays. For 1968 and '69, the most powerful engine option was the famous Chevy "427." When ordered with a triple 2-barrel carb setup and external side-mounted exhaust pipes, the 427 packed a walloping 435 hp. With a single 4-barrel carb and rear exhaust, the engine still put out a thunderous 390 hp. For the single model year of 1970, the Stingray could also be ordered with Chevy's largest engine, the enormous 454 cubic-inch V-8. Power ranged from a mere 360 hp to a brutish 450 hp. Also in 1970, the Corvette replaced the standard 327 base engine with a 350 cubic-inch V-8, which still powers the current generation of Corvettes.

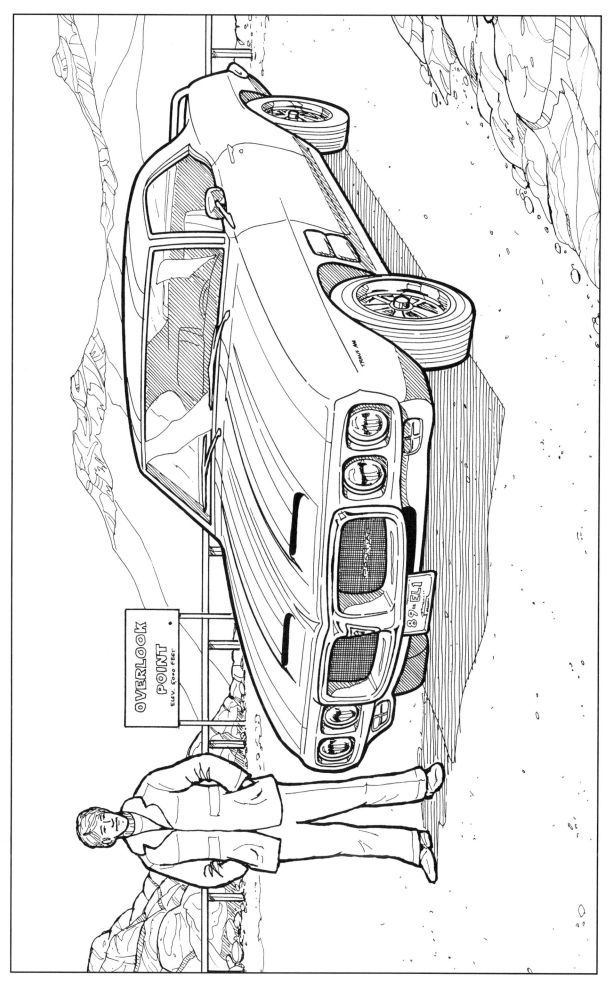

25. 1969 Pontiac Firebird Trans Am

Pontiac's Firebird pony car was offered in a special model, the Trans Am, beginning in 1969. Named after the Trans American road racing circuit, it featured special suspension to improve overall handling, as well as a white-only body color with dual blue stripes extending from the front of the hood to the trunk lid. It was powered by a Ram Air 400 cubic-inch engine producing 335 hp. For 1970, a 455 cubic-inch Ram Air V-8 became the standard Trans Am powerplant. The Trans Am went on to become one of the most successful pony cars ever marketed, with lower horsepower models in production well into the 1990s.

26. 1969 AMC Hurst/SC Rambler Scrambler

American Motors developed the compact-size Rambler American model into a pocket rocket with the 1969 "Rambler Scrambler." This little 2-door hardtop was powered by a massive 390 cubic-inch V-8 putting out 315 hp. Fitted with an eye-catching red, white, and blue paint scheme and a large carburetor air scoop mounted on the hood, the Rambler Scrambler boldly announced its presence at stoplight drag races. Built only for the 1969 model year, a restored Rambler Scrambler can command a respectable price in the current classic car market.

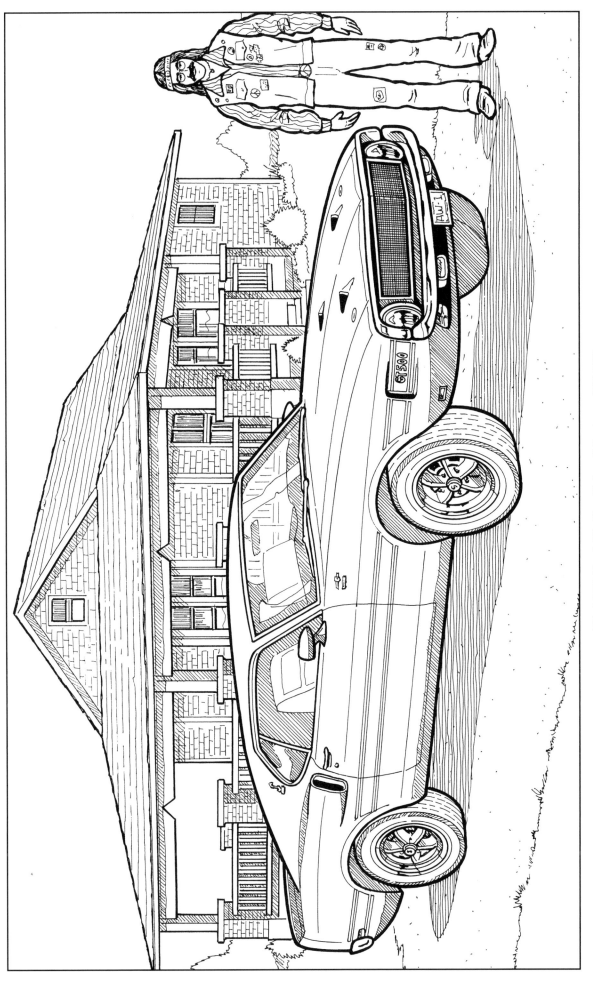

27. 1969 Ford Shelby Cobra Mustang GT-500

The specially modified Shelby Cobra Mustangs were created by Texas race car driver and builder Carroll Shelby. First introduced for 1965 in the GT-350, the Shelby Cobras had special suspension, roll bars built into the interior, double shoulder-harness seat belts, and a highly tuned 289 cubic-inch V-8 generating 306 hp. The GT-500 was introduced in 1967, powered by the massive 428 cubic-inch "Cobra Jet" engine fueled by twin 4-barrel carburetors. Although the horsepower was advertised as 335, most auto experts believe it was closer to 400. The Shelby Cobra was the top of the Mustang muscle car lineup and one of the premier vehicles of that era.

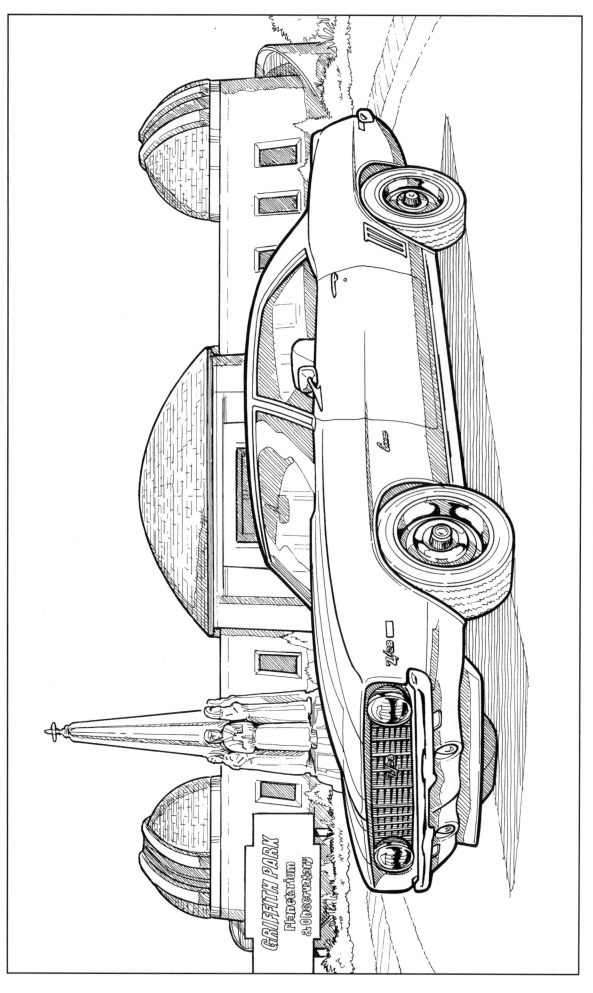

GRIFFITH PARK
Planetarium
& Observatory

28. 1969 Chevrolet Camaro Z/28

Just as Chevrolet answered the Mustang with the Camaro, the manufacturer designed the Z/28 version to compete with both the Shelby Cobras and Camaro's sister vehicle, the Firebird Trans Am. Brought out in 1967, the Z/28 used a highly modified 302 cubic-inch V-8 tuned to produce an advertised 290 hp, a figure most enthusiasts considered unrealistically low. A limited number of Z/28s were created for 1968, powered by a 302 powerplant equipped with dual 4-barrel carburetors and generating 350 hp. For 1970 the Z/28 received a new 350 cubic-inch engine putting out 360 hp. The Z/28 version of the Camaro was a major sales success within the muscle car field.

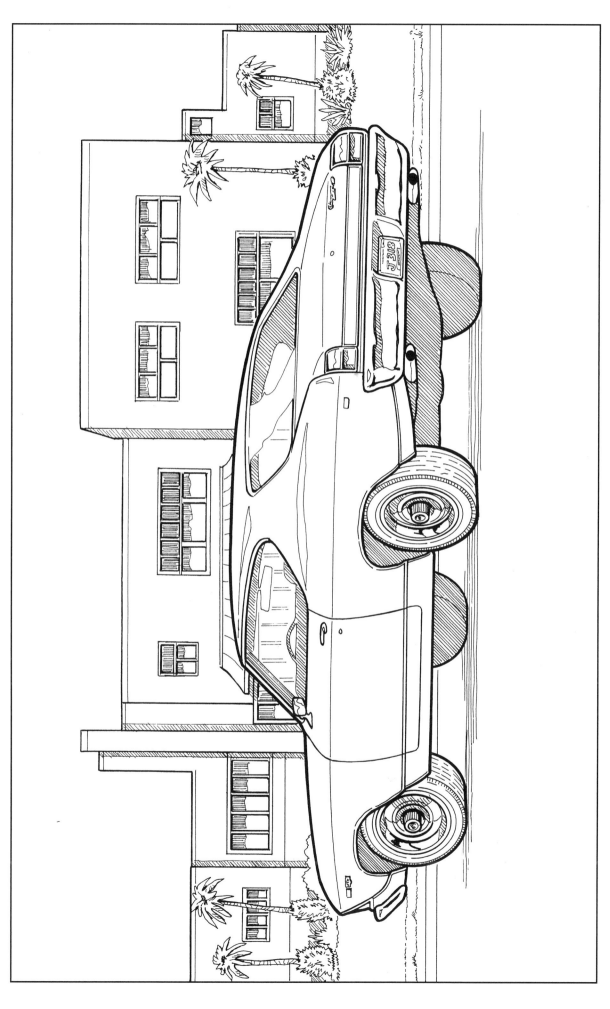

29. 1969 Chevrolet Chevelle Malibu SS 427

A limited number of 1969 Chevelle 2-door hardtops were built, without the SS badges and trim but equipped with the mighty 427 cubic-inch V-8. The mid-size Chevelle body combined with the 425 hp engine created a monster of a boulevard racer. Extremely rare in today's classic car market, a 427 Chevelle demands a top selling price. For 1970 the Chevelle SS was offered with a massive 454 cubic-inch engine developing 375 hp. The Malibu was one of the models offered in this line.

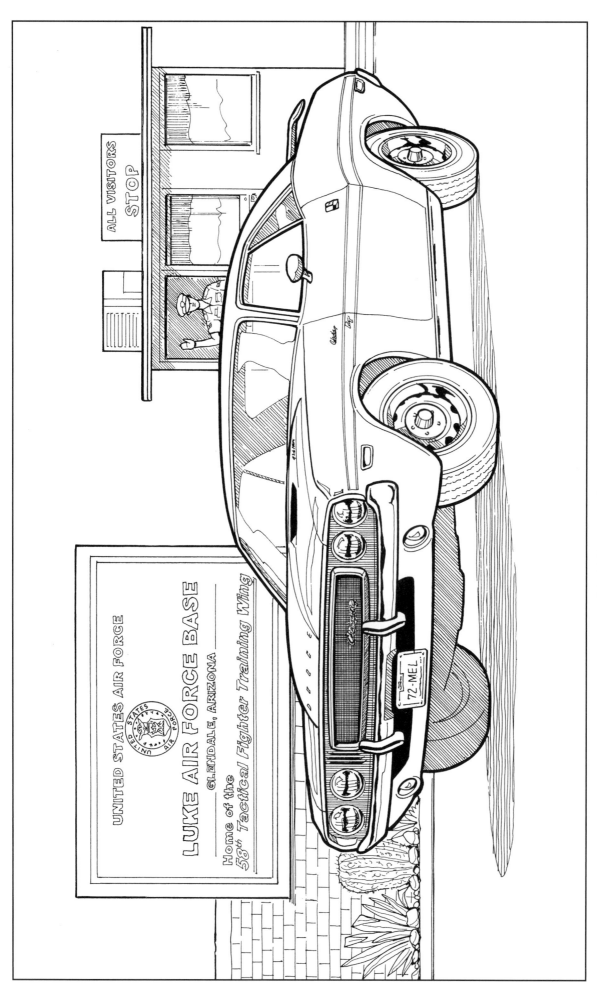

30. 1970 Dodge Challenger R/T

In 1970, the Dodge division of Chrysler introduced a potent entry in the "pony car" muscle series—the Challenger R/T. Its sleekly styled body could be equipped with a variety of optional engines. At the low end was the 340 cubic-inch V-8 putting out 275 hp. Next up in power was the venerable 383 cubic-incher rated at 335 hp. The biggest displacement engine offered was the monster 440 cubic-inch V-8.

This powerplant could be fueled by either a single four-barrel carburetor or three two-barrel carbs—the "six pack" option—with ratings of 375 hp and 390 hp, respectively. The "baddest" Challenger on the street, however, was powered by Chrysler's legendary 426 "hemi," pumping out a massive 425 hp. Few muscle cars of the era could keep up with the Challenger in all-out acceleration.

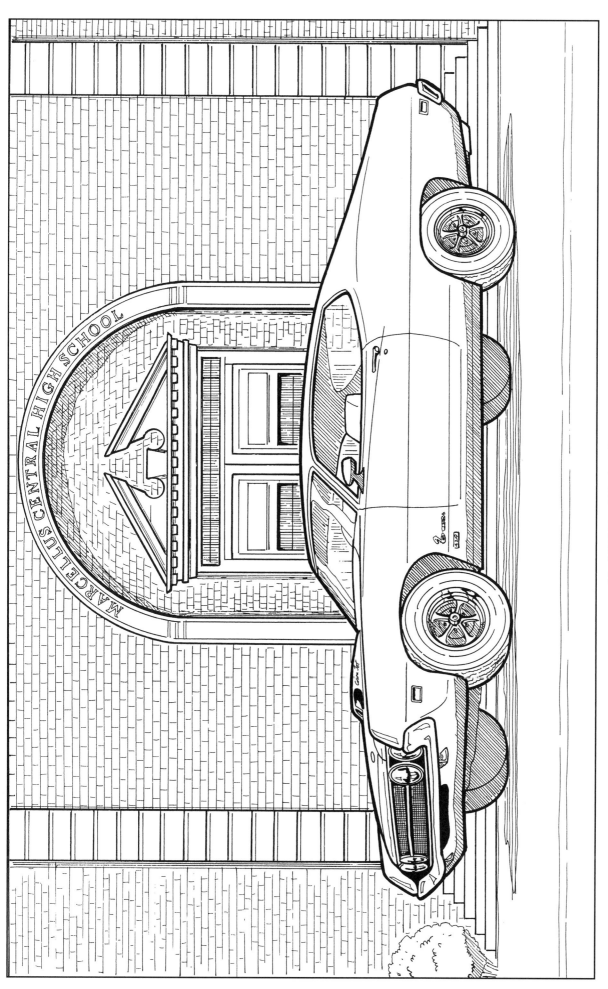

31. 1970 Ford Torino Cobra

The Torino fastback depicted above was based on the mid-size Ford Fairlane sedan. The Fairlane first joined the muscle car ranks in 1966, when the 500 XL model was equipped with a potent 390 cubic-inch, 335 hp engine. For 1966 and '67, a small number of Fairlane 500 XLs were built with a 427 cubic-inch V-8 producing an enormous 425 hp. By 1968, the Torino version of the Fairlane was available powered by the 428 Cobra Jet engine, rated at 335 hp. The 1970 Torino Cobra pictured above carried the powerful 429 Cobra Jet powerplant with its impressive 370 hp.

32. 1970 AMC Rebel Machine

American Motors followed up the Rambler Scrambler of 1968 with the red, white, and blue "Rebel Machine" of 1970. Based on the larger Rambler Classic body and frame, it was powered by a 390 cubic-inch, 340 hp V-8. A large hood scoop provided ram air induction for the single 4-barrel carburetor. Incorporated into the hood scoop was an externally mounted tachometer to register engine RPMs (revolutions per minute, the measurement of engine speed). The Rebel Machine was offered only for 1970, making it quite rare on today's classic car market. AMC's lone entry in the muscle car market after the Rebel Machine was their stylish pony car, the Javelin.

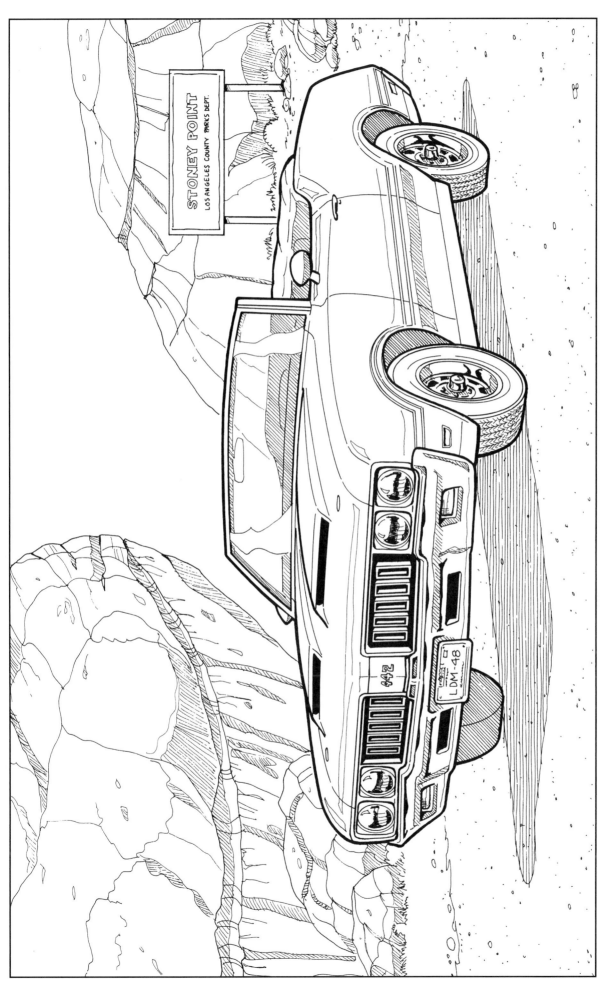

33. 1970 Oldsmobile 442

The Oldsmobile division of General Motors jumped into the mid-size muscle car arena in 1965 with an optional package featuring a 330 cubic-inch, 310 hp engine. By 1966 the offering moved up to 400 cubic-inches and 345 hp. A triple 2-barrel carburetor version was also available with 360 hp. In 1970, the 442 model shown above featured a 455 cubic-inch V-8 churning out a respectable 365 hp. A limited number of "Hurst/Olds" 442 models were built with a 455 engine modified to put out a tremendous 450 hp.

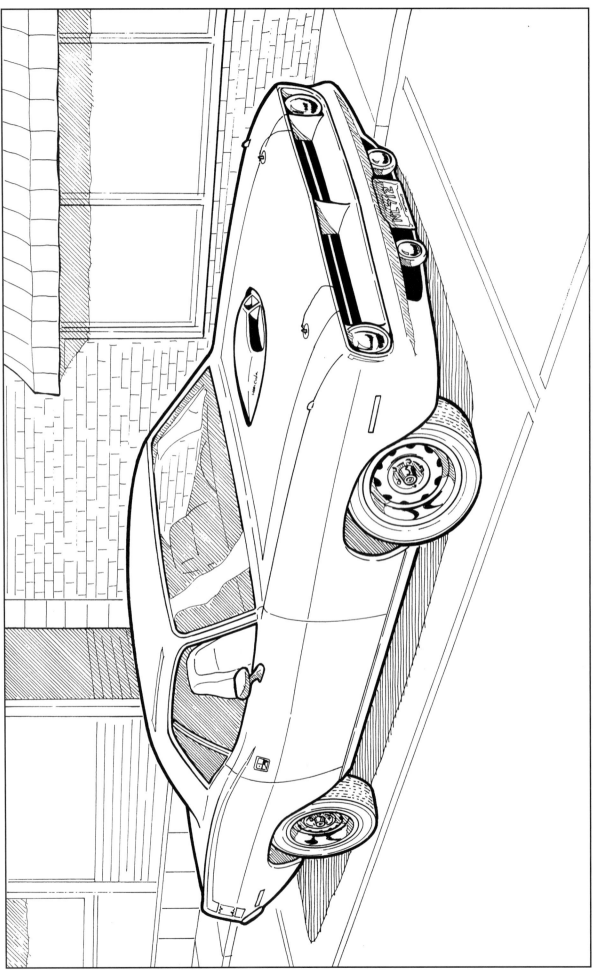

34. 1970 Plymouth "Hemi-Cuda"

Chrysler's pony car entries were the Plymouth Barracuda and Dodge Challenger. Muscle car versions of these vehicles were powered by a number of big Chrysler engines. The Barracuda could be equipped with a 340 cubic-inch, 275 hp engine, or a 383 cubic-incher putting out 335 hp. Top of the line engines for 1970 were the brawny 440 cubic-inch V-8 with a single 4-barrel carb rated at 375 hp, and the 440 fueled by three 2-barrel carbs—the famous "six pack"—generating 390 hp. But the meanest Barracuda on the block was the brutish "Hemi-Cuda," powered by the legendary 426 "hemi" engine pumping out 425 hp.

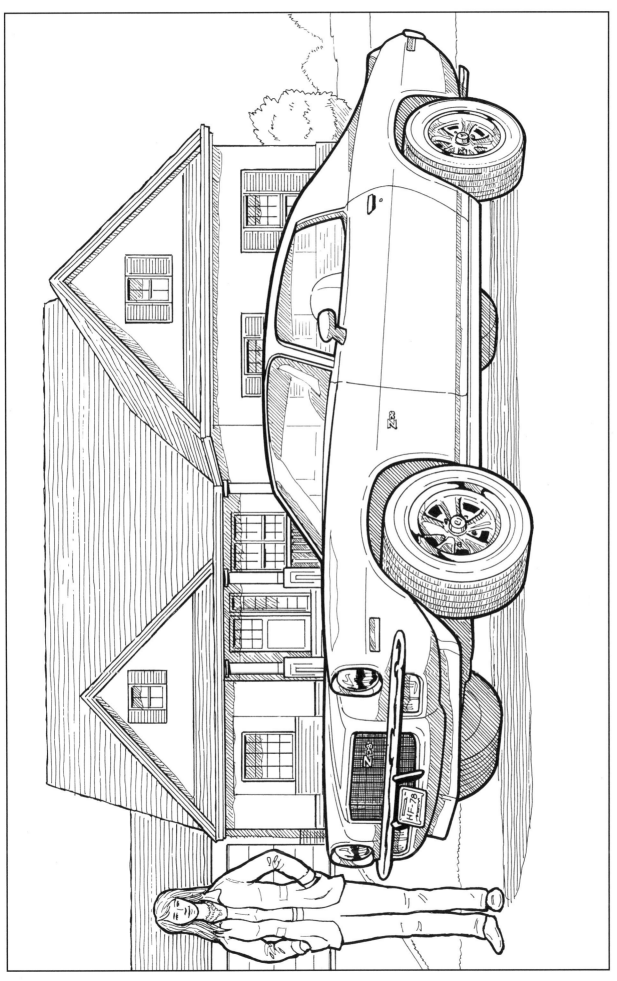

35. 1970 Chevrolet Camaro Z/28

The Camaro line received a major restyling in 1970. The distinctive "European" look introduced that year has now become one of the most sought after of the classic Camaro models. This stylish pony car was powered by a 350 cubic-inch engine producing a hefty 360 hp. The Z/28 became the best-selling Camaro muscle car over the vehicle's long production history.

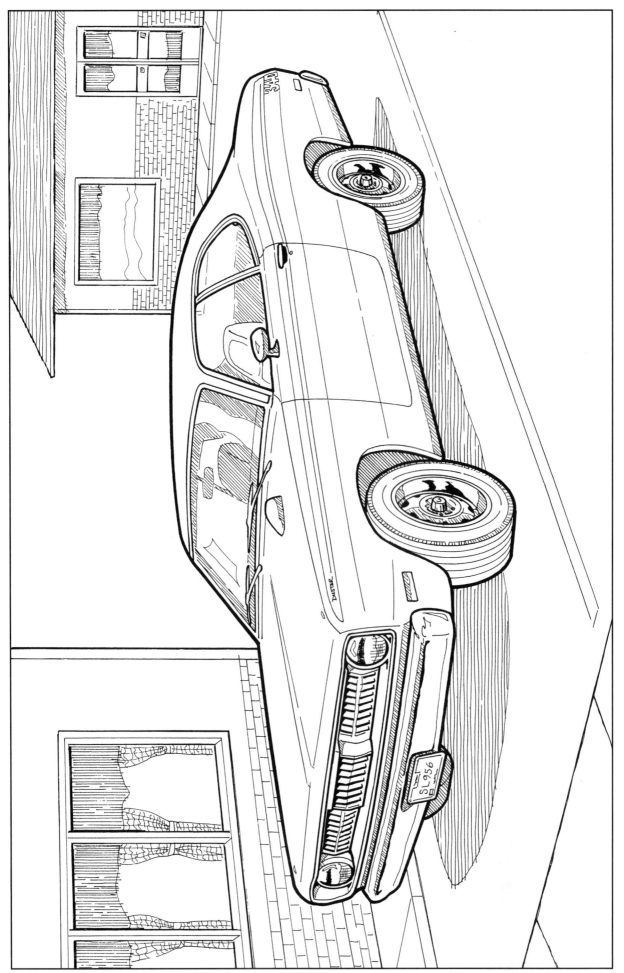

36. 1970 Plymouth Duster

The Duster was Plymouth's entry in the compact division of the muscle car market. It was built as a 2-door hardtop on the low-priced Valiant sedan chassis. Equipped with the muscular 340 cubic-inch, 275 hp V-8, the Duster competed with the Chevy Nova SS350 and its Chrysler sister vehicle, the Dodge Dart Demon. A hood-mounted tachometer was an option on both Chrysler compact muscle machines.

37. 1970 Buick GSX

To compete with Pontiac, Oldsmobile, and Chevrolet in the mid-size muscle market, Buick introduced the GS series in 1968. The models offered that year were the GS 350 and GS 400, both designated by their engine size in cubic inches. The smaller GS 350 engine was rated at 300 hp; the larger GS 400 pro-duced 345 hp. The GSX version came along in 1970 and was equipped with a massive 455 cubic-inch powerplant pumping out 360 hp. With carburetor hood scoops, rear-deck spoiler, and special paint striping, the GSX was one of the most eye-catching muscle cars of the era.

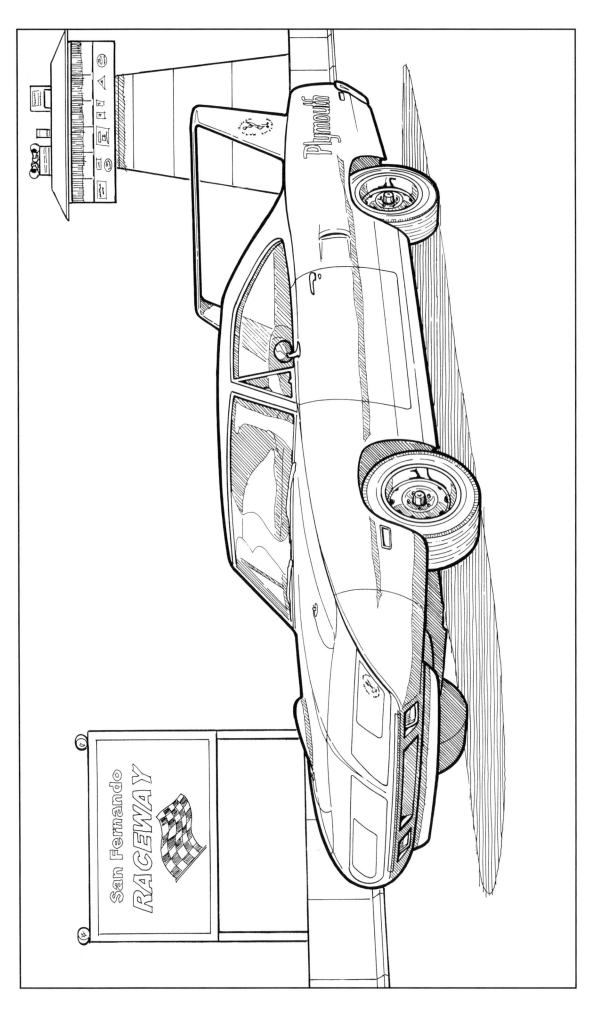

38. 1970 Plymouth Roadrunner 'Superbird'

There was no mistaking the identity of the high-winged Plymouth "Superbird" or its cousin, the Dodge Daytona. Nothing on the highway even resembled their distinctive profiles. Built to qualify for NASCAR competition, the vehicles featured an aerodynamic, wind-cheating steel nose cone that added 18 inches to the length of the car. At the other end, a huge air spoiler was mounted high on the trunk lid to create downforce for extra traction at

high speed. The street versions could be equipped with either the 390 hp, 440 "six-pack" engine, or the 426 "hemi" with 425 hp. Both racing gimmicks actually worked on the track. The Superbird and Daytona did so well in the 1970 NASCAR season that they were restricted in competition the next year. Produced only in 1970 and '71, these vehicles are now quite valuable on the classic car market.

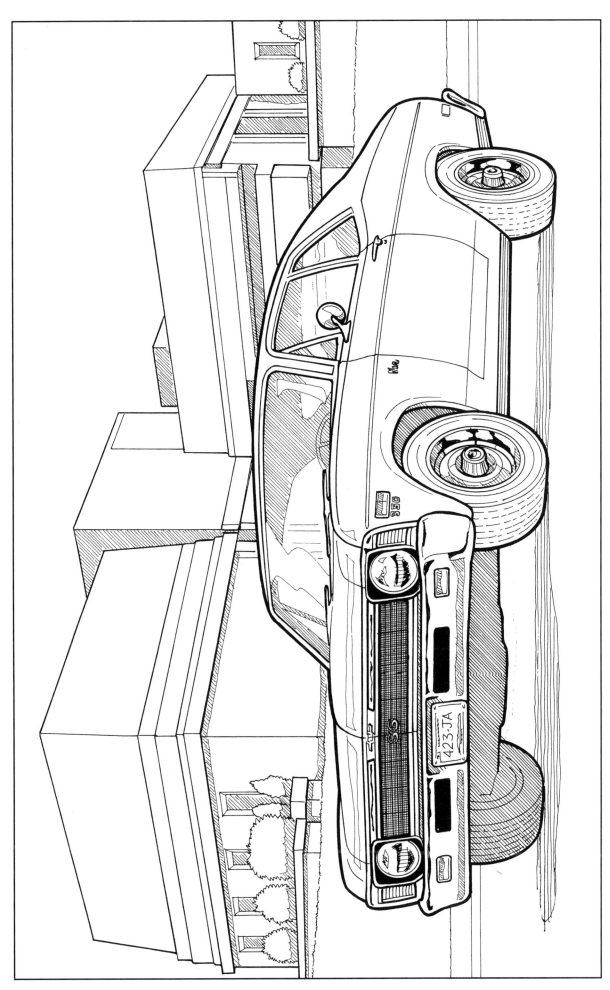

39. 1971 Chevy Nova SS 350

The affordable, popular Chevy Nova Super Sport (SS) series were fast, compact muscle cars. Originally based on the Chevy II compact car introduced in 1963, the Nova SS models were available with a variety of powerful V-8 engines. The 1964 version was powered by the venerable "283" cubic-incher rated at 280 hp. For 1966, the 327 engine was offered with 300 hp. The most potent Nova was the SS 396 of 1968. This 375 hp V-8 made the little Nova one of the fiercest street-racing competitors. The 1971 model depicted above was equipped with the dynamic 350 cubic-inch Chevy engine that pumped out 270 very respectable horses.

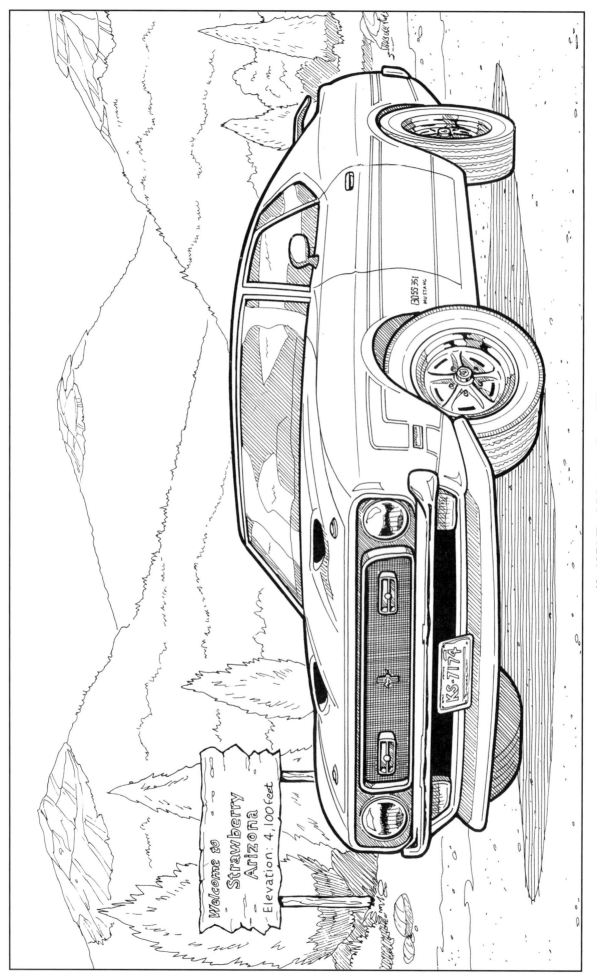

40. 1971 Ford Mustang Boss 351

Ford offered a new series of muscle cars, the "Boss" Mustangs, beginning in 1969. The Boss 302 Mustang featured a highly tuned 302 cubic-inch V-8 developing 290 hp. Equipped with front and rear spoilers, hood scoops, and distinctive body striping, the Boss 302 looked ready for the racetrack. Also available in 1969 and '70 was the Boss 429, considered by many to be the fastest production Mustang ever built. The 429 cubic-inch powerplant was officially rated at 375 hp, but many experts think the actual output was closer to 500 hp. Because only a small number of Boss 429s were built during the 2-year production run, a restored model can fetch a very high price on today's classic car market. For 1971, Mustangs were offered in the Boss 351 version with a 351 cubic-inch V-8 putting out 330 hp.

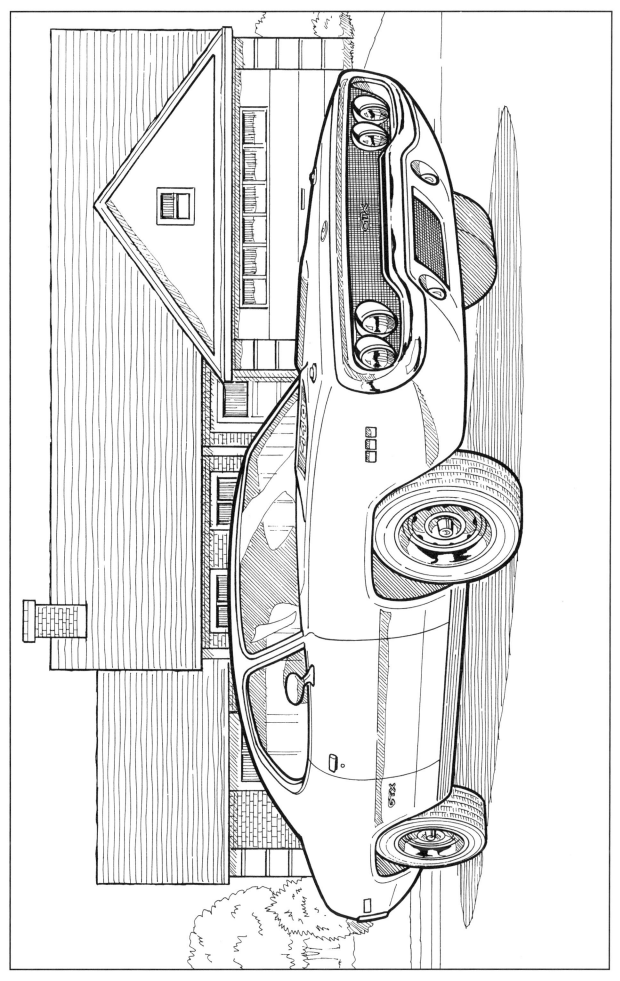

41. 1971 Plymouth GTX

The Plymouth division of Chrysler offered a mid-size muscle car beginning in 1967. The GTX was a 2-door hardtop based on the Belvedere family sedan chassis. Equipped with more standard and luxury features than the stripped-to-the-bone Roadrunner, the GTX could be ordered with the 440 "six-pack," putting out 390 hp, or the monster 425 hp, 426 "hemi" engine. The last production year for the GTX was 1971, foreshadowing the gradual close of the muscle car years by 1975.

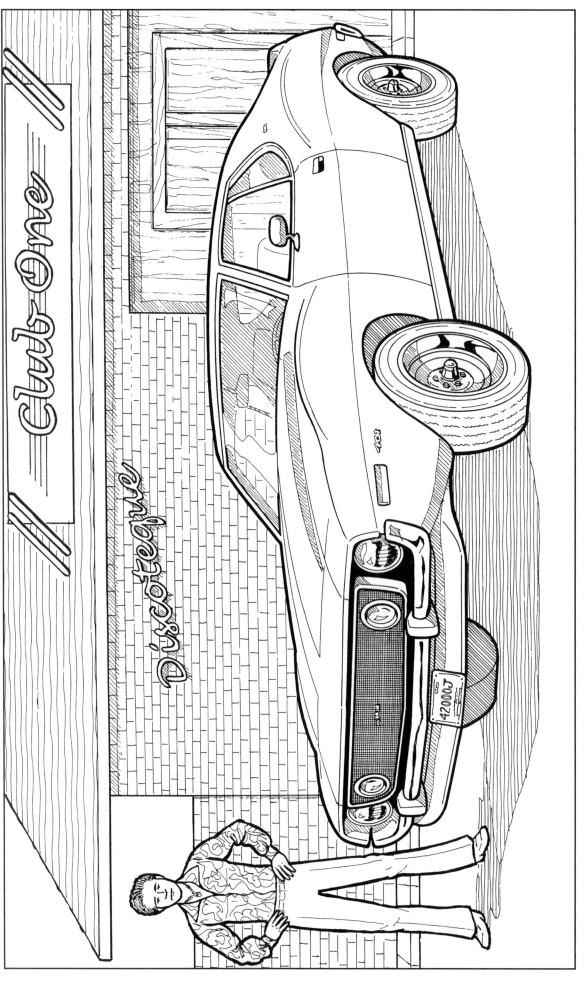

42. 1973 AMC Javelin AMX

American Motors offered the Javelin as its pony car beginning in 1968. Several muscle car versions were produced, including the SST model, offered from 1968 to 1974. Initially, the Javelin could be equipped with a 290 cubic-inch, 225 hp V-8, or a 343 cubic-incher with 280 hp. In 1970, the 343 was increased to 360 cubic-inches and 290 hp. In 1973 the Javelin AMX muscle car model was introduced; it could be powered by a 390 cubic-inch V-8 generating 315 hp, or a 401 cubic-inch powerplant yielding 330 hp. The Javelin was produced until 1974. Although it never racked up the sales figures of the Mustang or Camaro, it was a solid member of the muscle machine club.

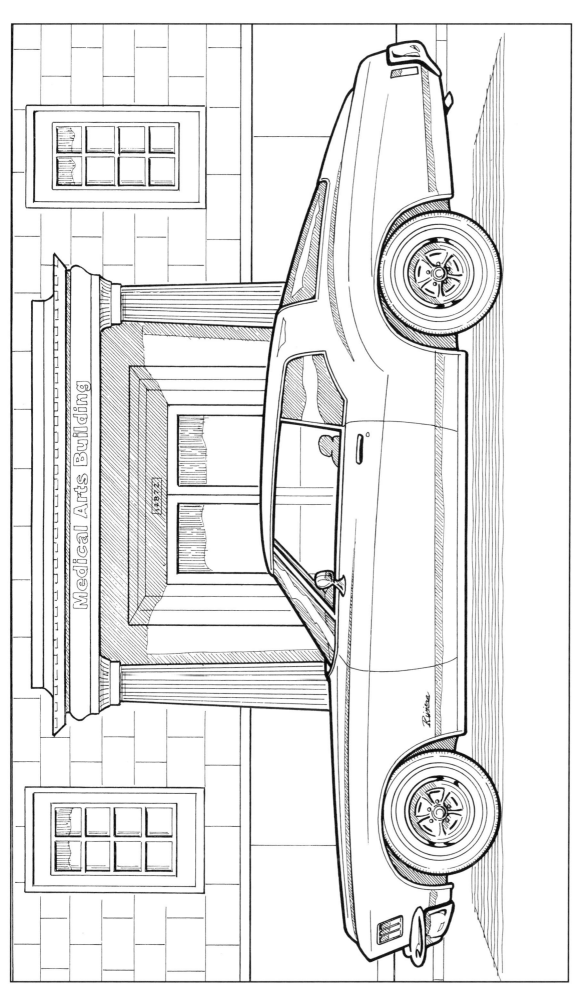

43. 1973 Buick Riviera

Returning full circle to the early years of full-size muscle cars, the Buick Riviera was a beautifully styled personal luxury vehicle with lots of power. With a wheelbase of 122 inches and weighing over 4,000 lbs., the Riviera was a cousin of the Chrysler 300 series and the big Chevy Impalas and Ford Galaxies of the early 1960s. The Riviera GS was equipped with a muscular 455 cubic-inch V-8 pumping out 330 hp. This engine could move the massive vehicle from 0 to 60 mph in just 8.4 seconds. For greater fuel economy and in response to emission requirements, the standard 455 was modified; the 1973 Riviera's horsepower dropped to 250 hp (standard) and 260 hp (GS). The distinctive pointed front end and "boat-tail" rear were designed by Bill Mitchell, head of auto styling for General Motors. The Riviera's elegant appearance distinguishes it as one of the most beautiful muscle cars ever created.

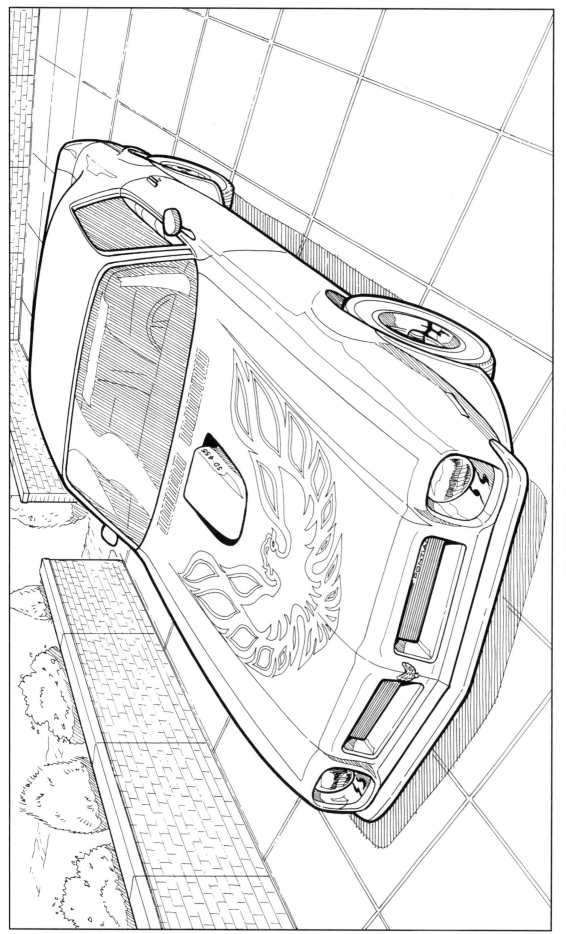

44. 1974 Pontiac Firebird Trans Am

The muscle car era ended in the mid-seventies as a result of several factors. The decrease in Middle East oil production during the early 1970s caused a shortage of gasoline and other fuels, resulting in gas rationing throughout the United States. In addition, tough government regulations mandated lower exhaust emissions, and the big-engined, gas-guzzling muscle cars lost their appeal to the majority of automobile buyers. Car builders responded by discontinuing a number of models and reducing horsepower in the remaining muscle machines. The 1974 Firebird Trans Am pictured above was still powerful and fast, but its real muscle was greatly reduced. The big 455 cubic-inch V-8 was detuned to 290 hp, down from the potent 370 hp of several years earlier. Although the most popular of the muscle machines, such as the Mustang and Camaro, remained in production throughout the 1980s and '90s, they were shadows of their stunningly fast former versions. By 1975, the uniquely American era of the muscle car had gradually drawn to a close.